From Gliders to Rockets

by Sarah Jane Brian

Table of Contents

Introduction

Up, up, and away! In 1783, two brothers from France showed off a new invention. It was the first hot air balloon.

Joseph and Etienne Montgolfier (mon-GOLF-ee-ay) filled their balloon with hot air and smoke. A crowd watched as the balloon took to the skies. It flew over a mile.

Later, the brothers flew another balloon. Hoisting a rooster, a sheep, and a duck into the air, the balloon flew two miles.

The Montgolfier brothers' hot air balloons were painted blue and gold.

Soon, two men took a ride in one of those new flying machines. People could fly at last.

Hot air balloons were fun to ride in. But balloons were hard to steer. People needed better ways to fly.

In 1804, Sir George Cayley assembled the first **glider**. A glider has wings like an airplane. But it has no engine. It uses wind to float through the air.

Another pair of brothers read about the glider. Their names were Wilbur and Orville Wright. The brothers would soon build their own aircraft.

In the 1890s Otto Lilienthal made his own gliders. He took more than 2,000 flights.

Chapter 1
The Wright Brothers

In 1899, Wilbur and Orville Wright ran a bike shop in Ohio. But the two men had a dream. They wanted to build a flying machine.

The Wright brothers read all about flight. They learned about other men who built flying machines.

Soon, the brothers began thinking of how to build a better glider. No one had ever built a glider with controlled steering. Wilbur had an idea. He wanted to try bending the tips of the wings. He thought that might help him steer the glider.

Building bicycles in this workshop may have helped the Wright Brothers think of ways to build aircraft.

Orville, left, and Wilbur, right, almost always wore suits and ties.

In July 1899, the men built a small glider. It had a wingspan of 5 feet (1.5 meters). It flew like a kite. A person on the ground held strings attached to the wings. The strings bent the glider's wings to control how it flew. Wilbur's idea worked.

The Wrights decided to build a larger glider. This time it would carry a man.

Wilbur and Orville worked on their new glider for months. They looked for a place to test it. They needed lots of strong, steady wind. The perfect place turned out to be the beaches of Kitty Hawk, North Carolina.

Try, Try Again

In 1900, Wilbur and Orville arrived at Kitty Hawk. The beach was windy, sandy, and empty. It was perfect for test flights.

The Wright brothers built new aircraft for the next three years. They came back to Kitty Hawk to test their designs every summer.

At first, the gliders were unstable and hard to control. But Orville fixed the problem.

Next, Wilbur and Orville built their own engine. In 1903 they arrived at Kitty Hawk. There they would test a new aircraft with an engine. They called the aircraft the *Wright Flyer*.

Soon the weather grew cold. But Wilbur and Orville were too close to give up now. On December 14, the brothers were ready. They tossed a coin to see who would make the first flight. Wilbur won. The *Wright Flyer* took off. But then the plane fell onto the sand.

Next, it was Orville's turn. On December 17, 1903, he started up the *Wright Flyer's* engine. The plane climbed into the air and flew 120 feet (36.5 meters). This was the first time that someone flew a plane with an engine.

Orville takes his historic first flight as Wilbur watches. The brothers flew three more times that day. Each flight was longer than the last.

Chapter 2
Heroes of the Skies

The Wright brothers kept working. By 1908, they built a plane that could fly 100 feet (30 meters) high. It stayed in the air for an hour.

The Wright brothers began selling their planes. Other inventors built planes, too. Flying races and contests became popular. Many planes crashed. But pilots still wanted to fly.

This plane crashed at a flying contest. There were a lot of crashes in the early days of flight.

The Red Baron

In 1914 World War I broke out. Airplanes were an important part of the war. The most famous pilot was Baron Manfred von Richthofen. He was from Germany. His plane was painted bright red. People called him the "Red Baron." He shot down 80 planes during the war. The Red Baron's plane was shot down in 1918.

The Red Baron flew this plane during World War I.

Cal Rodgers was the first person to fly across the U.S. He made the trip in 1911. It took him 84 days. Rodgers crashed many times. He had to replace almost every part of his plane.

Harriet Quimby was the first female pilot in the U.S. In 1912 she flew 23 miles (37 km) across a body of water in Europe. She was the first woman to make the trip. Rodgers and Quimby were famous.

Charles Lindbergh stands next to the *Spirit of St. Louis* before his historic trip.

Charles Lindbergh

Charles Lindbergh was one of the greatest heroes of flight. He was an unknown pilot in 1927. That year, he decided to fly from New York to Paris, France. No one had ever done this. If he could make it without stopping, he would win a prize.

Lindbergh's plane was called the *Spirit of St. Louis.* The plane was small. Lindbergh didn't carry a radio or a **parachute**.

Lindbergh had to fly more than 3,500 miles (5,600 km). He needed a lot of fuel. That made his plane heavy. When the plane first took off, it flew very low.

Lindbergh sat in this small cockpit during his $33\frac{1}{2}$-hour trip. His only food was a bag of sandwiches and some water.

Lindbergh had to fly in the right direction to Paris. He used a magnetic device called a compass. The points of a compass are north, south, east, and west. A needle on the compass shows which way is north. This helped Lindbergh travel east across the Atlantic.

Lindbergh had to fly through fog and ice. But he had a bigger problem. Lindbergh couldn't sleep the night before his trip. Now it was hard to stay awake.

Lindbergh flew for $33\frac{1}{2}$ hours. At last he arrived. He was the first person to fly alone for such a long distance. More than 100,000 people came to watch him land.

The trip made headlines in newspapers everywhere. Millions of people applauded Lindbergh at a parade in New York City.

Amelia Earhart

Amelia Earhart was a famous pilot. She was the first woman to fly alone across the U.S. She also set many speed records.

Earhart was the first woman to fly alone across the Atlantic Ocean. She made the trip in 1932. Earhart ran into bad storms on her trip. Some of her equipment broke. At one point, her plane suddenly dropped toward the ground! But Earhart landed safely.

People all over the world thought Earhart was very brave. "Please know that I am quite aware of the [dangers]," she wrote. "I want to do it because I want to do it. Women must try to do things as men have tried."

Earhart was the first person to fly alone from Hawaii to California. Thousands met her plane.

Amelia Earhart poses with the plane she tried to fly around the world.

In 1937 Earhart took off on her last trip. She planned to fly around the world. Sadly, she never made it. Her plane was lost over the Pacific Ocean. No one ever found Earhart or her plane.

The Hindenburg Disaster

Large airships traveled the skies in the 1920s and 1930s. They were called **zeppelins**.

Zeppelins were filled with a kind of gas. The gas made the airships float. But the gas burned easily. On May 6, 1937, an airship called the *Hindenburg* caught fire. It crashed to the ground. Many people died.

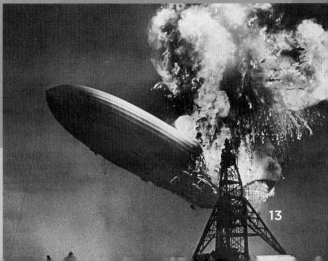

Chapter 3
Flying in World War II

The United States entered World War II in 1941. Airplanes became very important.

Faster planes were needed to help win the war. So designers worked quickly to build faster planes. The new planes could fly more than 400 miles (640 km) per hour.

In 1944, a new German fighter plane took to the skies. This plane could fly 550 miles (885 km) per hour. It was the first jet fighter.

Benjamin O. Davis led the first African American fighter pilots.

World War II airmen often decorated their airplanes.

Older planes used spinning **propellers** for power. Newer jets don't use propellers. Instead, a jet engine mixes air with burning fuel. The jet blasts the air out of the back of its engine. This pushes the plane forward. Most planes today have jet engines.

Breaking the Sound Barrier

After World War II, pilots wanted to fly faster than **Mach I**, the speed of sound. No one knew if it was possible.

Chuck Yeager wanted to try. In 1947, Yeager sped through the air in a plane with a rocket engine. Yeager flew the plane at 700 miles (1,100 km) per hour. He had passed Mach I!

Chuck Yeager named his plane *Glamorous Glennis* after his wife.

In 1953, Jackie Cochran flew faster than the speed of sound. She was the first woman to fly that fast. Cochran was a native of Florida. She set 69 flying records.

Chapter 4

To Space and Beyond

Scientists had a new goal after World War II. They wanted to go into space.

In 1957, the Soviet Union launched *Sputnik*. *Sputnik* was the first manmade **satellite**.

Explorer I took off in 1958. It was the first U.S. satellite. Next, the U.S. wanted to send a person into space. But the Soviets were first. They sent Yuri Gagarin into space in 1961.

The U.S. was not far behind. U.S. **astronaut** Alan Shepard blasted off into space just weeks later.

These were America's first astronauts.

Astronaut Ed White walked in space.

Project Apollo

Project Apollo was another step in the journey to the moon. Early Apollo flights got close. Then came the most exciting flight of all. It was time for astronauts to land on the moon.

Apollo 11 blasted off in 1969. A few days later, Neil Armstrong stepped out onto the moon. He spoke to Mission Control in Houston, "That's one small step for man, one giant leap for mankind."

Armstrong and Buzz Aldrin planted a U.S. flag on the moon.

A Space Center

In the 1960s the Johnson Space Center (JSC) was built in Houston, Texas. It is the center for all human space flight activities.

Today astronauts are trained at the Johnson Space Center in Houston. They practice living in space suits. They learn how to scuba dive and how to jump in a parachute. Every astronaut learns how to deal with emergencies.

JSC is also the home of mission control. All communication from space goes to Mission Control in Houston.

An astronaut experiences zero gravity at the Johnson Space Center.

Conclusion

Brave people have explored the skies for hundreds of years. Some people rode in balloons. Others floated in gliders. And still others flew in planes. Over the years people flew farther and faster. Finally they traveled into space.

Spacecraft without anyone on board have traveled to Mars. Scientists keep learning more about space with each trip. Someday they hope to send people to Mars.

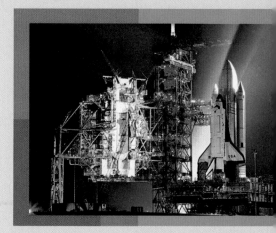

The space shuttle *Columbia* blasts off on April 12, 1981.

Mae Jemison became the first African American woman in space in 1992.

Important Dates in Flight

1783 — First flights in hot air balloon

1804 — Sir George Cayley invents first glider

1903 — Wilbur and Orville Wright pilot first powered, controlled flights

1914–1918 — World War I fought. Planes play important role.

1927 — Charles Lindbergh flies across Atlantic Ocean

1932 — Amelia Earhart flies across Atlantic Ocean

1937 — *Hindenburg* explodes

1939–1944 — World War II fought. First jet fighters appear.

1947 — Chuck Yeager flies faster than speed of sound

1957 — Soviet Union launches *Sputnik*

1965 — Johnson Space Center opens

1969 — Neil Armstrong and Buzz Aldrin land on moon

1981 — Space shuttle *Columbia* blasts off

Glossary

astronaut *(AS-truh-nawt)* a person who travels into space *(page 17)*

glider *(GLIGH-duhr)* an aircraft that flies without a motor by riding on air currents *(page 3)*

Mach 1 *(MAHK WUN)* the speed of sound, faster than 650 miles per hour *(page 15)*

parachute *(PAR-uh-shewt)* a piece of equipment that allows a person attached to it to be dropped from an airplane and float slowly and safely to the ground *(page 10)*

propeller *(pruh-PEL-uhr)* a device with blades that spin like a fan, creating force by pushing against air *(page 15)*

satellite *(SAT-uh-light)* an object that orbits around Earth, the moon, or another large body in space *(page 16)*

zeppelin *(ZEP-uh-lin)* a large airship filled with a lightweight gas that makes it float *(page 13)*

Index

Comprehension Check

Summarize

Use a chart to record clues about the author's perspective. Then write a sentence stating the author's perspective. Use the information in the chart to summarize the book.

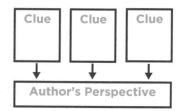

Think and Compare

1. Look back at page 7. What does the author tell you about the Wright brothers' character? *(Author's Perspective)*

2. How do you think Charles Lindbergh might have felt as he flew across the Atlantic? Use facts from pages 10–11 to support your answer. *(Analyze)*

3. Early pilots and astronauts were heroes to people all over the world. Identify a public person today who is a hero to you. Why do you admire this person? *(Apply)*